No
Stopping
Place

No Stopping Place

LETTERS TO MY GRANDCHILDREN
ON THE GOD I'VE COME TO KNOW

Mary Virginia Parrish

PROVIDENCE HOUSE PUBLISHERS
Franklin, Tennessee

Copyright 2000 by Mary Viriginia Parrish

Printed in the United States of America

04   03   02   01   00   1   2   3   4   5

Library of Congress Catalog Card Number: 00-109106

ISBN: 1-57736-209-8

Cover design by Gary Bozeman

Cover art Image Club Graphics

PROVIDENCE HOUSE PUBLISHERS
238 Seaboard Lane • Franklin, Tennessee 37067
800-321-5692
www.providencehouse.com

To my daughter
Ann Carter McDonald
mother of Allen and Virginia
with love

There is no stopping place in this life—

no, nor was there ever one for any man, no matter how far along his way he'd gone. This above all, then, be ready at all times for the gifts of God and always for new ones.

—*Meister Eckhart*

Contents

Acknowledgments

A Heart Full of Thanks

to all who have impacted my life for good, beginning with my parents

to countless ones whose speaking and writing have challenged me to be more than I am

to the many prayer groups of which I've been a member

to John and Carol Waters for the use of their Florida condo for a brief respite

to The Other Marys and the Discipline and Discovery groups for giving me the joy of leadership while being led

to my spiritual guides from Dr. Frank C. Laubach to Father Niel Jarreau S.J., and Father Augustine Moore, OCSO

to Marianne Cox without whom this book would have never reached completion. For your countless hours typing, retyping, editing, and for the gift of your friendship, I thank you, Marianne.

Introduction

Virginia and Allen,

INTENTIONS, GOOD THOUGH THEY MAY BE, ARE SOMETIMES sidetracked. So it has been with my plans of special letters to you. In these intervening years, Allen, you have graduated from Wake Forest and are now attending Emory University Medical School. Virginia, after recently spending a semester in Florence, Italy, where you studied art history, you are now back at Vanderbilt completing your junior year. As for me, I am spending a few weeks in Venice, Florida, in the lovely condo of John and Carol Waters. Their graciousness allowed me freedom to return to this long-neglected writing project.

Starting over again is never easy. Only a strong sense that God nudged me to this writing keeps me going. Voices of inspiration and discouragement are vying with each other, all within my own mind. How dare I seek to write about God given how little I know. Yet, I am quick to respond: God desires to be known, else why would God have made the invisible visible in Jesus?

St. John wrote that he had seen and touched Jesus; I can make no such claim. However, I have experienced God's presence, and I will tell you only of that which I have heard and seen for myself—no secondhand reporting.

My doubts have been many; my search has been long. My struggle to know God has been persistent. And all is used. God gathers all those questions and then says, "Look. See what I am doing. Listen. Hear what I am saying."

"Open my eyes that I may see," has become a constant refrain of my heart. Glimpses of truth are certainly all that I have been given, but those glimpses assure me that knowing must be shared.

As you read, you will discover that speaking about my spiritual experiences has been difficult. The old set of cultural norms in which I was raised discouraged speaking of personal things, and certainly your relationship with God is the most personal of all. (Later, I'll write to you about the time when I was forced into sharing.) Once these old cultural impediments were knocked down, I was set free. Now, it is with ease and great joy that I say: this is the God I've come to know.

During those years between imprisonment and freedom, I would hear a word spoken through me, and then I would have to live it out—to make the word flesh. This was the case with my young college friend Jimmy. Jimmy had agonized over the untimely death of his young and beautiful mother only to suffer a second grief a few years later when his father died. Late one evening, Jimmy's passionate search for answers drove him to your grandfather, Cliff, and me. He poured out his doubts, his anger, and his total rejection of his childhood faith. He wanted some light, some comfort for his troubled spirit. We listened with understanding and love. In the early morning hours, I said, "Jimmy, I cannot prove to you that there is a God, but I would stake my life on it." I had made a risky statement and hoped I could live up to it if tested.

Only one week later, I received a long-distance call from Jimmy. "Mary Virginia, you know I love you and don't mean to be cruel and insensitive, but I must ask, how do you feel now?" Jimmy had just learned of my husband's sudden death from a heart attack. "Jimmy," I replied, "by faith I believed the words I spoke to you, but now I know. The reality of God's presence has been so powerful that I cannot deny it. Like a mother tenderly holding her firstborn, God has held me, all the while assuring me that all will be well."

So, my dear grandchildren, what I am writing is what I have had disclosed to me. Although grateful for the many years of teaching I've had about God, it has only been through firsthand encounters that I can say I *know*. This arduous search, this seeking, this asking, this knocking is a quest that has no end. There is no stopping place in the spiritual life. Nonetheless, I have discovered this journey home to be the one thing that keeps life exciting and heaven inviting.

with all my love,
I write these letters to you.
Grandmother

witness

Good morning, children,

HOW FORTUNATE YOU ARE TO BE ALIVE IN SUCH A TIME AS this, to attend the ending of the twentieth century and the beginning of the twenty-first; to be attentive to what is happening, alert to the opportunities; aware of the One who created the evening and the morning and called it day.

In these letters, I want to tell you what motivates your grandmother and about the One who is the motivator. For years, I had known *about* God and even taught Sunday School classes. But to *know* God is vastly different—not to say that my knowing is complete. Yet through the years, there have been little hints, little whispers, little glimpses of light that have made the difference in my life between darkness and light, death and life.

Why do I choose to do this now, you may ask. Partly because of time. At the age of eighty-six one begins to wonder: How long, Lord? Partly because we never seem to find *time* or *stillness* (the right opportunity?) to talk about those things that are eternal. I've always dreamed of leisurely sharing with those I love these things of the Spirit, but somehow we never get around to it. We are too busy with the immediate—the tyranny of the urgent. There are too many competing demands; we're too restless to be still. One does not just plunge into such a discussion. It requires a certain climate: a receptive mood, or a sense of quiet listening. Then, there is a timidity in all of us that prevents us from talking about the things that matter most, strange people that we are.

Do you recall Thorton Wilder's play *Our Town*? Remember the scene in the cemetery? Dead persons are lined up in chairs. The stage manager is in charge. Emily, who died in childbirth, asks permission to return to earth for just one day. After much pleading, she is granted her request. She returns to her old home. Excited over the prospects, she suffers great frustration shortly after her arrival. Before she asks to return to her place in the cemetery, she reveals the cause of her frustration. She says to the stage manager, "We don't have time to look at one another." Then she sighs, "I didn't realize all that was going on, and we never noticed. Do any human beings ever realize life while they live it? Every single minute?" The stage manager pauses and then answers, "No, the saints and poets may . . . They do some."

The question haunts me: Do any human beings ever realize life while they live it? I recall standing with a young bereaved husband at the side of his wife's casket. Looking down into her beautiful face, he commented, "She died before she ever learned to live." How tragically true. Living life fully can be done only when the Author of life is involved.

As a young person, I was taught that religion and personal matters were off limits in conversation. This attitude made it difficult for me to share my faith. Some years later, I was invited to speak at the World Day of Prayer in Mayfield, Kentucky. The subject for the day was You Shall Be My Witnesses. In my customary way, I prepared by gathering materials: Bible, books, etc. But thoughts refused to come. The word *witness* stymied me. I reached for my dictionary in hopes of finding some definition of the word that would let me off the hook. But, no. Witness refers to a firsthand encounter, giving an account of what you have seen or heard. No longer could I hide behind someone else's experience. I must speak of the God I knew. Painful though it was, it proved to be a real breakthrough for me.

With the way anything and everything is talked about in public today, I am sure it is hard for you to understand the reluctance of earlier generations to speak of religious beliefs. Hence, I cannot tell you what my parents believed. They were wonderful, moral people. By faith, they followed the Scriptures as best they knew them. I am proud of their integrity and character. They were faithful in church attendance and participated as teachers and elders but never discussed their beliefs.

As children, we went to Sunday School and church every Sunday morning and night, every Wednesday night prayer meeting, and any special revivals. If you were too sick to go to Sunday School and church, you had to take castor oil. In my youth, it was a cure-all. Allen, if all your new medicines fail when you start practicing, you might try it! It will kill or cure. Awful stuff!

Hospitality was one of my parents' gracious gifts. For Sunday dinners (at noon), we often invited a minister or visiting missionaries. We children were free to invite our friends. Jokes were made about preachers and fried chicken, for that was a sure dish for Sunday. Yes, children, we had fried green tomatoes too, but those were mostly served for breakfast along with sausage or bacon, eggs, and biscuits with homemade damson preserves.

Having preachers join us at our large, round oak table was always fun for me. Much to the embarrassment of my parents, I would ply them with theological questions, which ofttimes were never answered to my satisfaction. I asked questions like: "Can people in heaven see us down here?" (you can see I was still thinking of a three-layered universe) and "If they can, how can they be happy when we are so bad and there is so much sorrow?" A deeper question came later: "What does 'I AM THAT I AM' mean?'"

I thank God for having been brought up in a church that gave me the risky freedom to wander all over the place theologically. The Christian Church (Disciples of Christ) has no stated creed. It separated from the Presbyterian Church on the question of open communion. The founders, Thomas and Alexander Campbell along with Barton Stone, came to the strong conviction that communion should be offered to all believers. (Most churches agree with that today.) Baptism by immersion is practiced, and communion is served every Sunday. I took baptism quite seriously and believed strongly that immersion must be the form. As an elementary student, I found a Scripture on which to stand and tried to convert some of my Presbyterian friends during recess. Time has taught me that the amount of water is not important.

I am grateful that I grew up observing communion weekly. Although the preaching of God's word was extremely important, the Lord's table commanded the most significant place in the center of the chancel. As I've grown older and have a fuller understanding of the meaning of communion as a sacrament, I strongly believe that the church that fails to observe weekly communion is diminished in power and effectiveness.

For a seeker such as myself, it was good to have the freedom to question. However, I have come to believe that there is a false assumption in Christian education. It is true that as one seeks, asks, and knocks, one will find. However, I've learned that statements of faith set down by theologians who have studied, thought, and prayed through the fundamentals give one something to debate, defend, or reject. To me, that seems like a good spiritual exercise.

What I am writing you is my story—my spiritual journey from childhood beliefs through times of much questioning and discarding, to the rediscovery of Jesus and a maturing faith. I am trying to be as honest as I know how, but, of course, my journey will not be yours. Each must discover God, or more accurately, each must place himself or herself before the Creator of the universe and discover that he or she is loved—dearly loved—and called by name. Ours is a very personal as well as universal God whose name is Love.

Faith grows slowly day by day as one practices God's presence. Each of us starts with a tiny seed. As that seed is watered and tended, it grows. In the last forty years, my faith has grown strong and matured. It has become secure in the knowledge that God's way will be victorious. As I confess to you all my ups and downs and the roundabouts of my journey, my knowledge of God is still limited. But let me witness to you, dear grandchildren, the God I've come to know is sufficient to give me strength for today and hope for tomorrow.

Bless you, my dears.
Grandmother

Miracles

Dear Allen and Virginia,

GOOD MORNING! I WISH I COULD SEE YOU AND GREET YOU in person, but we'll have to let this letter suffice. Although I'd like to write you daily, it has not worked out that way.

Where to start? What does one say first about this mysterious being we call God, this unseen One whom Jesus called Father? Jesus even gives us the privilege of calling God *Abba* (Daddy), which makes God seem not so far removed, not so remote. As a child, there was a picture in my mind of a very stern judge, all-seeing and non-feeling, who tabulated every good and every bad deed in a huge book. I feared it was heavy on the debit side for me.

How different is my image of God now. What must precede any divine-human relationship is the reality that God is alive, active, and can be met. Even though I didn't ever quite believe to the contrary, I confess that for years I thought of God as retired. I knew that God was in the beginning and would be at the end of time, but where I was, God wasn't.

Some years ago, a couple of theologians wrote a book entitled *God Is Dead*. I did not dare go to this extreme, but somewhere along the way, the thought that God rested on the seventh day (as the Bible says) and was still resting remained with me. We poor humans were to pick up the work and continue what God had started. As an activist, I tried to do my part and saw this as my role for many years. It took a personal tragedy to change this concept in my mind.

My first baby, Cliff Parrish Jr., died. After three days of intense labor, when I should have had a cesarian section, the baby was forcibly removed. (At that time, c-sections were not performed after a certain point in the natural delivery.) The little fellow, a perfect eight-pound, four-ounce beautiful baby boy, was too exhausted from trying to be born. He died a few hours after birth. Mangled in the process, I was not expected to live.

After all the preparation, all the plans, all the dreams I had over those long nine months, I was left with only an empty cradle, a damaged body, a broken heart, and staccato-like questions: why, why, why? If God were all powerful, if God were all loving, why did this happen to my baby? If God were . . . on and on and on.

For weeks, those questions persisted. Then a little book was placed in my hands. I don't even remember the title, but its author was E. Stanley Jones, a well-known missionary to India. Among the many words in that book, two leaped off the page: *why*, and *how*. I realized that I must not continue thinking "Why?" but "How?" *How* can this heartrending experience be used to bless others? *How* can my brokenness become healing for others?

Two years later, I was four-and-a-half months pregnant with your mom and visiting my sister in Paris, Tennessee, when I lost all the fluid surrounding the fetus. Dr. McSwain, our family doctor, told me I would lose the child. Again, I felt that awful pain—why? Cliff was away serving in the Navy; he and I so wanted a baby. I had forgotten that earlier lesson and was again asking *why*.

Anger made me question the goodness of God. Allen and Virginia, what I am going to relate may be hard to believe, but this is what happened.

By God's grace, before I knew the meaning of that word, I was able to change my prayer to one of surrender—*not my will, but thine.* Even as those words were said through me, I rationalized as to what they meant. Basically, I would not allow myself to be bitter, no matter what happened. The moment those words—and not my will—were silently uttered, I encountered God. Please don't think I saw a man with a long, white beard or even an angel. I saw nothing, at least not with my human eyes, but I saw God. More accurately, I knew God was alive, real, and present.

The thrill of that disclosure is beyond description. *God is . . .* a present tense God; not just was, as in the beginning, not just will be, as at the close of the age, but *God is.* The very hereness, nowness, isness of God flooded my soul with joy. Completely forgetting the realities of my physical condition, I was enfolded in love; I was suspended in wonder. Why had I not been told? Did anyone else know? How could it be? An ordinary woman such as I. The finite and the Infinite meet. Wonder of wonders.

When that sacred moment passed (how long, I know not, for there is no time in that dimension), a voiceless Voice told me that my baby would live. This was in spite of the fact I was having labor pains at four and a half months.

In a day or two, I asked that Dr. McSwain be called to reexamine me as I became aware that embryonic fluid had once again encased my baby. At first, he refused, but later that afternoon curiosity won out. He came to my sister's home and examined me. Never shall I forget the expression on his face or his words, "My God, it has." There is a letter from that doctor in your mother's baby book to prove it.

The Holy Spirit began to teach me that the miracle was not the safeness of my baby, but the encounter, the surrender of my will. The outward sign is the manifestation of an inner happening. That instruction set me on a new path. I had always been trying to change the outer— the environment, the people, the society. Now, I was told that that which happens in the heart is the important thing. The spiritual journey is an inner journey.

Back home, where I was brought by ambulance, I was required to stay in bed for four months. After years of rejecting that which is termed a miracle, I wondered if I could ever make anyone understand what had happened. Timidly, I talked to my minister about the experience. He thought I was confused. My efforts to communicate were feeble and futile. I found no one who could emphathize. Time passed. Ann Carter Parrish was born by cesarian section on June 28, 1945. What a joyful day and what a joy she has always been since then.

Over time, I almost lost a sense of that encounter. That happens when we have no one with whom to share. Like other skeptics, I even began to doubt the experience. Six years later at a Christian Church conference in Murray, Kentucky, a tall man stood up to speak. From the moment he began to pray, I knew that he knew the One I had encountered briefly. Dr. Frank C. Laubach spoke with such compassion as he told about the people of the Philippines and the illiterates around the world. It was he who created the Each One Teach One literacy program which has spread throughout the world and is in great use even today under the Laubach Literacy Program.

His words—and much more than his words, his intimate relationship with Jesus—created a hunger within me such as I had never known. I yearned for such a relationship. At one time, I would have been impressed by Dr. Laubach's credentials (his doctoral dissertation was later used by Woodrow Wilson in writing the charter for the League of Nations), but now his accomplishments were not what made an impact on me.

The word was *relationship*. That was the key—not the conduct, not a creed, but relationship, participation in a life. The Holy Spirit spoke to my heart and said I, too, could have such intimacy if I were willing to pay the price. I'm willing, Lord. A covenant was made.

All that weekend, I literally clung to Dr. Laubach. Seeing my hunger and recognizing my need, he gave me a copy of his little *Game with Minutes*, which outlines a pattern for learning to pray without ceasing. Dr. Laubach also urged me to attend a Camp Farthest Out. These ecumenical, non-denominational retreat camps were founded by Dr. Glenn Clark for the purpose of teaching persons to pray as Jesus prayed. The goal was that a chain of loving prayer groups would ultimately encircle the globe, encouraging peace and harmony among people.

Dr. Laubach became my mentor. Through our correspondence, attending camps where he spoke, his visits to my home, and reading all that he had written, I drank in his teaching on prayer. Like any art, prayer requires daily discipline. I had always thought of prayer as a gift, yet it must be learned. However difficult, I knew I must start on this journey, this journey of learning to live in the awareness of God.

That was the beginning. Grateful for the early foundation I had received from home and church, I was now on a new exploration. I was on a search that has taken me many miles and many years. It is the inner search all pilgrims must make once God becomes real, and they answer, YES.

I love you and will always be praying for you whether I am here or there. Really, it is all here!

Grandmother

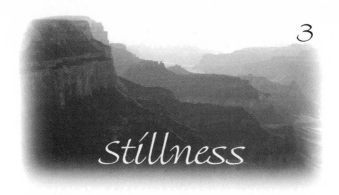

stillness

Dear children,

TOO GROWN UP TO BE CALLED CHILDREN? YOU'LL ALWAYS be children to me, much-loved children. Don't ever forget that. But more important than my love is that of your heavenly Father, the One who calls you beloved and whose love is limitless and eternal. Let me suggest that each morning you take a few moments to think on God's love for you. There is nothing you can do that will either diminish or increase that love. God is love; God can do no other.

This morning the bay of Venice is a picture of tranquility. Even though boats of every description ply these intracoastal waters, at this early hour there is no movement. The sailboats line the curves of the land like little soldiers. Behind them are Monopoly-size houses. The smoothness of the water allows the boats, the houses, the palm trees to be reflected. If nature, which is one of life's greatest teachers, is correct, I reflect that upon which I gaze as well.

No wonder the saints of old instruct us to behold God. As we look upon God's unhurriedness, we become still within. God works in stillness and in silence; both are required if we would learn to pray. After having met with hundreds of groups and individuals, I am convinced that becoming still is the most difficult and yet the most essential of all the spiritual disciplines. Ridiculous, you say? Anyone can be still. However, *inner* stillness is not learned quickly. Try it for fifteen minutes a day.

"I hope it doesn't take me that long," was the response of a young woman who was visiting with me to chat about things of the Spirit. I had told her that it took me one whole year to become still, inwardly still. Dr. Laubach told me to start each day by being still before the Lord for fifteen minutes. This addition to my routine necessitated getting up even earlier than my husband and I usually arose. Nevertheless, my desire was so strong to have what he had that I was willing to follow Dr. Laubach's direction. Despite the pressures of constant travel and the demands of his literacy program, he possessed a serenity such as I had never seen.

In *The Spiritual Life*, Evelyn Underhill, a British writer much respected for her spiritual depth, wrote that St. John of the Cross said that every quality or virtue that the Spirit produces in a person's soul has three distinguishing characteristics, as if it were a threefold trademark: tranquility, gentleness, strength. Those marks were evident in Frank Laubach. However, acording to his *Letters of a Modern Mystic*, they were not natural to him. It took years of learning to be still, of learning to pray. His struggles are recorded in this personal diary.

"How did you get that stillness?" I asked another Frank, Frank Olmstead, a saintly Quaker. Like Dr. Laubach, his answer was the same: "Take time in quietness before the Lord." I could have been given no harder assignment, but I tried and tried and tried.

For one whole year, I battled the inner voices that hounded me to get up and do something—my many responsibilities like the scout meeting that afternoon, the person I must call, the program I had to plan for Church Women United. These screaming voices were so strident and persistent that it was impossible to be still. In desperation, I started keeping a notepad by my chair to jot down the most urgent requests. Then I would return to my futile attempts at stillness. Just wasting time, the voices cried, adding guilt to my already turbulent state.

Just think on the Lord, I was told. Think? My thoughts were jumping from one subject to another like the squirrels chasing each other outside my patio door. Finally, I decided to use a picture of Jesus on which I could focus. His eyes were penetrating, his invitation indisputable as I studied his face. For me, this was helpful but not the answer.

After working at this discipline for a year with no apparent success, I decided that I was going to prove this a futile exercise if something did not happen soon. I was attending a Camp Farthest Out where Dr. Laubach was a speaker, and although morning meditation was on the schedule, my determination drove me to get up even earlier to have my private time with the Lord. While meditating on Psalm 46, I came to verse ten. In giant letters, or so they seemed, the words jumped off the page and into my heart: BE STILL. I never got beyond those two words. For the first time in my life I knew stillness, inner stillness.

Every muscle, every cell of my body, every organ that was usually spastic, all were still. Words can never describe that experience. So still was I that "I" seemed no longer present. I was caught up in something wider, higher, deeper. In an awesome way, I became one with the universe. Never have I known such stillness; never since then have I not known the true meaning of stillness. Edna St. Vincent Millay's *Renascence* came to my mind, words that had thrilled me, but now I could identify. Her conclusion:

The world stands out on either side
No wider than the heart is wide;
Above the world is stretched the sky,—
No higher than the soul is high.
The heart can push the sea and land
Farther away on either hand;
The soul can split the sky in two,
And let the face of God shine through.
But East and West will pinch the heart
That can not keep them pushed apart;
And he whose soul is flat—the sky
Will cave in on him by and by.

How gracious of God to give us such moments of unspeakable joy. Why are such experiences given to some and not to others? This question was posed to me by members of the first prayer group to which I ever belonged. I shared their wonder, but perhaps the words of Saint Joan might help. In George Bernard Shaw's play, *Saint Joan*, the enraged king yells at Joan: "Why don't the Voices speak to me? I'm the King, not you." Joan replies, "They do speak to you, if you would listen. At the time of Angelus, you listen, cross yourself and hurry off. If you would stand and listen to the bells after they stop ringing, you would hear them, too."

We miss so much from our failure to listen, to listen to what God is saying to us. In his well-known book, *Celebration of Discipline*, Richard Foster says that hurry is one of the reasons only a few ever hear God speak. Along with hurry, Foster adds crowds and noise as weapons the enemy uses to keep us from God. Since most of us are bombarded by all three, there must be an intentional warfare against them. Making time in our cluttered lives for quiet before God is essential to the spiritual life.

Thomas Keating, a Trappist monk, has brought to the attention of the reading and praying public the power of "centering prayer." I was fortunate to attend a weekend at the Monastery of the Holy Spirit in Conyers, Georgia, where Fr. Keating conducted a workshop on centering prayer. He recommended focusing our thoughts on God for two twenty-minute periods a day. We began the period with reading a short bit of Scripture or some inspirational writing in order to quiet ourselves and allow ourselves to enter God's presence slowly and deliberately. If our minds wandered, we were to bring our thoughts gently back to God. At the end of twenty minutes, we were to pray ever so slowly the Lord's Prayer.

You may ask, since you had that experience of stillness a number of years ago, is it yours today? Let me hasten to assure you the answer is no. The rare moment of stillness—of insight—is a gift not to be preserved in a holy shrine, but to give impetus to our daily relationship with God. Stillness continues to be difficult for me. I have to practice it daily. Each day I must start over as if it were the first day of my journey. Unlike other forms of knowledge, spiritual learning is not accumulative.

Let me caution you. Spiritual disciplines are of no value within themselves. They simply place us before God who does the transforming work. God works in silence, not shouting to be heard. Through spiritual disciplines, we must learn to be still. For me, there is no cost too great, no amount of time too valuable to experience God's gift of stillness.

Bless you, Virginia and Allen,
Grandmother

solitude

Dear Allen and Virginia,

THIS MORNING I'M THINKING OF SOLITUDE. SILENCE, stillness, and solitude form a holy triad. Each has its essential place in the spiritual life. When we look at Jesus our guide, we always see him practiced in inward orientation, inward listening, and inward silence. He was continually in communion with the Father. Regardless of his outward activity, inwardly he was listening and obedient to the Father's wishes. Jesus had so completely surrendered his life to the Father that he spoke only what God told him to say; he did only what he saw his Father doing. It is a moment by moment discipline—keeping our thoughts turned to God.

This surrender is not something we do once, and it's done. At first, it seems impossible, but as we practice God's presence, we begin to recognize that we are given the ability to so order our lives that we can think on two levels at once. We can be conscious of the presence of the Most High God even while listening to a person who has come for guidance. We need to form habits that help us become settled in this new way of continuous prayer. Often, a Psalm or poem or prayer memorized and prayed often during the day helps us become established. A prayer by Charles de Foucauld, founder of a movement known as The Little Brothers of Jesus, is a good selection to start the day. It is a meditation based on Luke 23:46. I include it for your use.

THE PRAYER OF ABANDONMENT

Father, I abandon myself into your hands;
Do with me what you will.
Whatever you may do, I thank you
    I am ready for all
    I accept all.

Let only your will be done in me,
    and in all your creatures.
    I wish no more than this, O Lord.

Into your hands I commend my soul;
    I offer it to you
with all the love of my heart,
    for I love you, Lord,
    and so need to give myself,
to surrender myself into your hands
    without reserve,
and with boundless confidence,
    for you are my father.
                    Charles de Foucauld

I've always been curious about what makes people tick. Some seem able to juggle a number of different jobs or activities while remaining calm and composed. In his *Living the Message*, Eugene Peterson writes about busyness being an illness of Spirit. That's it. We are too busy doing many things but accomplishing very little. Being busy has become a status symbol in our society. But Jesus demonstrated a different way. Even though he came to save the world, he was never too busy to stop and heal the blind man who called out. He was never too busy to take the little children in his lap and love them while talking about the Kingdom. Interruptions usually bother us, but Jesus was not living by our agenda. He used those times for teaching, for healing, for demonstrating. Oh, if we could only master that which the Master mastered.

We experience the pressures of always trying to be perfect, to produce, to fulfill the impossible expectations of friends as well as of ourselves. Jesus got his priorities straight in the wilderness. No longer did he have to control. There was a relation between his deciding and letting God the Father decide. When our own actions cease and divine action takes over, then that is the rest of which Jesus spoke—the lightness of burden—for the work is neither initiated nor done *by* us but rather, *through* us.

As I've studied persons who seem to have discovered the secret of living life in a serene way, I've come upon one characteristic that is common to all of them: they have ordered their priorities. They know what comes first. They are not tormented by decisions at each turn of events. It sounds so simple, yet simplification of life is not easily attained in our complex society. We need to make time for solitude, long periods of time alone with God in which to reflect, to examine. Socrates is noted for suggesting that an unexamined life is not worth living. I believe this is true.

As we read Scripture, we see that many persons had to spend long periods in the desert sorting things out, letting God reveal priorities. Think how long it was between Moses' call and his ministry. We know that the Spirit drove Jesus into the wilderness to wrestle with the enemy within and without. Which way should he go? How would he carry out the ministry assigned to him? Decisions had to be made. Jesus dealt with choices of position, popularity, power—choices that still hound each of us. Henri Nouwen spoke of the wilderness as the furnace of transformation. Surely the lesser things have to be destroyed in order to choose that which is paramount.

Solitude is a prerequisite for dealing with the questions: How am I going to live my life? Who makes the decision, this world, or God? I remember the first time I intentionally went into a wilderness, a retreat center of The Church of the Savior founded by Gordon Cosby. During that weekend, we had eighteen hours of solitude in which there was no conversation, no reading of books (even the Bible), no TV, radio, or newspaper. We say we long for such a time, yet when presented with it, we feel afraid and are uncertain about how to pray. The Hound of Heaven pursues us with deliberate speed, majestic instancy. Are we face-to-face with friend or foe? Aren't we foolish to think that the God who loves us with an everlasting love could ever be our foe?

For me, there came a time of solitude not of my own choosing. You remember my description of the loving way in which God held and carried me through the first days—even weeks—following Cliff's death. Then came the day God dropped me. I'm ashamed to confess that I found myself literally on the floor of my bedroom beating my fists like a spoiled child, crying out, "Where have you gone?"

"I am here," the answer came, "but I'll no longer carry you like a baby. You can wallow in self-pity and have others sympathize with you as a lonely widow, or you can get up off the floor and grow up spiritually. I want you to learn the blessedness of solitude. The choice is yours."

I chose the latter.

I love you,
Grandmother

Pentecost

5

Good morning, Allen and Virginia,

"EASTER WITHOUT PENTECOST IS A SPRINGTIME ABORTION," declared Fred Craddock at a retreat I was attending. That statement shocked us into rapt attention. It is understandable why he was voted one of the ten best preachers in the U.S.A.

Many of us base our beliefs on what happened at Easter and rightly so, but certainly the resurrection of Jesus is incomplete without Pentecost. Just as I have come to see Jesus still hanging on the cross, so have I come to agree with Dr. Craddock, a professor of homiletics at Candler School of Religion.

Our churches and we as individuals have neglected the study of the Holy Spirit. I speak as a mainline (whatever that is) Protestant who has gone to church all her life and has sat under the preachings of highly educated ministers. On my own, I have studied as a layperson. The Holy Spirit was tacked on at the end of prayers: God the Father, God the Son, and God the Holy Spirit (or Holy Ghost, which frightened me as a child).

As I dare to write of the Holy Spirit, I understand why the subject has been avoided. How can one put into descriptive words the wind, the light, the fire? These are the ways in which the Spirit moves. The wind cleanses, the light reveals, the fire burns. However, since these letters are about my journey toward God, I must share my experience with the third person of the Godhead, the Holy Spirit.

Knowing nothing about the Holy Spirit, I associated the Spirit with miracles, healing, speaking in tongues, and even casting out devils. As I write this, I realize I'm getting into deep water, but I promised I would be honest. I am not accusing the many wonderful preachers I have heard, nor am I blaming teachers and writers of the books I have read, but my knowledge of the Holy Spirit was zero. My ignorance and arrogance moves me with shame as I confess what I must.

Whether one receives the Holy Spirit at birth, at baptism, or later remains a source of great debate. For me, the fact remained, if I had the Holy Spirit, I didn't know it. Like the persons to whom Paul spoke at Ephesus (Acts 19:2), I had never even heard of the Holy Spirit. But this I knew: I had reached a point of knowing I needed more than I had. Further reading and further study were not the answers—I needed power.

With great skepticism, I visited some tent meetings. I must confess, I saw power. God was using these people more than some of the highly educated individuals whom I admired so much. Thus, the humbling process began. I searched in many places, and our loving God made me wait a long time before meeting my need. Blessed are those who are poor in spirit. Only when we recognize a sense of need can we come into that Kingdom of which Jesus spoke.

Being able to speak in tongues was the sign of the Holy Spirit in many of the places I visited. I questioned my reaction: Was I jealous of those who spoke so fluently with beautiful sounds which made no sense to me? Was I arrogant in thinking this gift unimportant, or were those who made this gift a requirement the arrogant ones? Reluctantly, I submitted myself to the embarrassment of asking for the baptism of the Holy Spirit at the hands of one who said glossolalia was the sign.

As this spirit-filled man placed his hands on my shoulders and prayed for me, God enveloped me in a great peace. To my knowledge, I did not speak in tongues, but that peace—that gentle pressure of hands on my shoulders—stayed with me for three days. God uses many different ways to show love. God knew how very much I was in need of a special touch, for it had been only six months since Cliff's death.

Some years later, a dear elderly pastor asked me, "Do you speak in tongues?" I was surprised, for at the weekend retreat I was leading there had been no mention of tongues. "Why do you ask?" I inquired. "Because there is something—a power—in your speaking that made me wonder if you had been baptized by the Holy Spirit."

I told him of my experience when I humbled myself and asked a person to pray for me to be baptized in God's Spirit. "I don't know whether it was the breaking of my pride or a new awareness and appreciation of the variety of God's children or what, but I have to recognize since that time, there has been a new power, a new way of speaking." The pastor seemed satisfied.

I recall another minister asking me about the Spirit. He had come to a Camp Farthest Out where I was speaking. As we chatted at the dinner table, he told me he had no sense of Christ living within him. I shared with him that I had come to realize that everything Jesus said for us to do is impossible. Since Jesus had told the disciples to wait until they were empowered before going out, this knowledge caused me to search for this same power through the Holy Spirit. I told him that as an adult, I had rediscovered Jesus. It brought tears to my heart as I looked at this highly trained, beautifully educated minister, for I saw the yearning in his heart. Then he asked, "How can I make that rediscovery?" "With the simplicity of a child, just say, 'Jesus, come into my heart,'" I answered. At the end of the evening session, he sent a message to me saying, "I did and He did."

During the last session of camp, it was with a new humility that this man came forward and confessed that for over thirty years, he had preached about God, but he did not know God. However, with childlike sincerity, he had invited Jesus into his heart, and He dwells there now.

It is good to know about God, and I can't over-emphasize the necessity for Bible study and the training of the mind. But it is a heart message that the simplest, the least educated can receive that makes the difference between knowing about God and knowing God.

I love you,
Grandmother

6

Prayer

Dear Allen and Virginia,

TODAY I WANT TO WRITE TO YOU ABOUT A FAVORITE subject of mine: prayer. Once I realized that it was the secret of Frank Laubach's and Frank Olmstead's lives, I started in a new direction. From studying and reading almost exclusively about social action—doing, doing, doing—I began a journey toward becoming, being.

Prayer is a gift, yet at the same time, it must be learned. In his daily reflections, *Living the Message*, Eugene H. Peterson writes that we need a long apprenticeship in prayer. And then we need graduate school; the Psalms are the school.

The Psalms are used by Trappist monks day after day during vigils, lauds, vespers, and compline. I asked my spiritual guide and friend, Dom Augustine Moore, who for twenty-seven years was abbot at the Monastery of the Holy Spirit, how many times they went through the Psalms. He told me that they pray all one hundred-fifty Psalms every two weeks. Please note that I did not say read or say, but *pray* the Psalms.

Wouldn't you get awfully tired of going over and over the same Psalms? We have forgotten one effect of repetition: you might hear something new. It is the intent of the spiritual to penetrate the secular until there is perfect integration: sacred/secular, earth/altar.

Most of our concept of prayer is, "Now I lay me down to sleep," our talking to God, and that is a wonderful prayer for children. Nevertheless, until we learn that prayer is not monologue but dialogue, we haven't really prayed. Strangely enough, we learn that God initiates; our prayer is but a response. Prayer involves listening, listening to God whose voice is not heard with human ears but with the heart. Cultivating a listening heart is absolutely essential if we are to commune with God.

Prayer is speaking and listening; it is thinking about God, and it is resting in God. Thomas Merton speaks of sacred reading as prayer. This notion pleases me since I had often wondered how one could pray without ceasing as we are instructed to do. Let's think together about the various forms of prayer. As we study the prayer life of Jesus, we discover that he used all those forms with the exception of confession, for he had no need to confess.

Confession is a good place to start. Protestants have not emphasized confession as much as Catholics. In his book *Life Together*, Dietrich Bonhoeffer has a chapter on confession that was the first to challenge me. The second was St. Ignatius of Loyola. In studying his *Spiritual Exercises* under the direction of a Jesuit priest, I found that St. Ignatius placed great emphasis on what he called the Examen of Conscience. He taught that the last thing before sleep should be a review of the day's happenings: reviewing the sins of commission and omission, confessing all that is contrary to our Lord's teaching, receiving forgiveness, and surrendering yourself into the arms of the loving, forgiving Father.

Meditation is a form of prayer spoken of in Psalm 1. The man was called blessed who meditated upon the law day and night. But, what is meditation? Sometimes we get strange pictures of persons who have to practice certain postures, but the important thing is missed. Meditation is chewing on, masticating, digesting. In the era of speed reading and with our hurried pace, we need to hold the Word in our mouths until, like a lozenge, it dissolves and reaches the innermost areas of our being.

Contemplation is a term often used interchangeably with meditation, but I differentiate the two in this way. Meditation centers the person in the presence of God, then God takes over and human effort ceases. One simply rests in God. Contemplation is not sleep, it is not mindlessness. Contemplation is quiet attentiveness to God.

Adoration is often neglected as a prayer discipline. I recall reading that Henri Nouwen had an interview with Mother Teresa and was expecting a long dissertation on what he should do. She quickly told him: just spend one hour a day adoring God, don't do anything you know is wrong, and go about your work. He was somewhat disappointed. Simply adore God. Some of the praise Psalms teach us this as well as worship passages such as Isaiah 6:1–8.

One way of praying without ceasing is through thanksgiving. Let me tell you about a lesson in thanksgiving I learned from my friend and helper, Martha. She was in the kitchen when I went in and told her of the many cards and letters that Ann Carter and I had received after Cliff's death and how thankful to God I was. Quickly Martha said, "Just keep thanking him. That's the way the blessings come." No learned preacher or theologian has given me wiser counsel.

In *Where Your Treasure Is*, Dr. Eugene Peterson stabs us awake to the power of intercession when he writes about the effect of prayer on social energy and political action: "Far more of our nation's life is shaped by prayer than is formed by legislation." I think of an intercessor as being God's go-between. What a tremendous challenge, what a wonderful assignment.

To many people, prayer means petition: Give me, heal me, help me. We all pour out petitions to God and rightly so. However, they are perhaps the least important, if there are degrees in arranging prayers. Supplication to God comes naturally; other disciplines must be learned and practiced.

Prayer unites us with God as nothing else can. I'm sure that my greatest teacher has been prayer, both alone and in groups. To neglect prayer is never to know God or self. John Calvin once said that to know God was to know self, and to know self was to know God, and it was hard to determine which came first.

It is said that there are no atheists in foxholes, which is true. However, God is one who wants to have communion with us all the time, not just when we're in foxholes. Learning to pray is learning to live.

Here's Life to you, my dears,
Grandmother

7

Weeping

Dear Allen and Virginia,

TODAY, MY MIND SEEMS TO BE FOCUSED ON THE WEEPING Christ. Allen, you were just a baby when I visited you and your family while your Dad was stationed in Guam serving as a doctor in the Air Force during the Vietnam conflict. How I anticipated that visit. The Christmas before had been so lonely that I dared make that long flight alone to spend the holidays with you.

The pilots spoke of the milk runs to Vietnam as just a matter of course. All was quiet until our president decided to go on the offensive. The B-52 bombers, called superfortresses, were based on Guam not far from your living quarters. Even the sight of them sent shivers down my spine, for in my heart I am a pacifist. Orders were sent out for bombs to be dropped indiscriminately, not only on military targets but also on schools, churches, homes, helpless women, and children. I remember the noise of those bombers taking off from the base nearby. Every half hour, waves of those huge planes took off shaking every inch of that little island. I shuddered that our nation was engaging in such violence.

I sought the comfort of God. I was reminded of Jesus praying over Jerusalem that "they might know the things that make for peace" (Luke 18:42). Nightly as I listened to that awful power leaving Guam on missions of destruction, I prayed for understanding and solace. The response seemed to say that these events would continue until all persons knew the things that make for peace and how to follow the way of the Prince of Peace, Jesus. Together, He and I wept over our world.

Another time I shared in the suffering of our Lord was in Peru. I was invited there to speak at a Camp Farthest Out, and my cospeaker was a Catholic priest. In his first talk, he chose as his text the prayer of Jesus as recorded in the seventeenth chapter of the Gospel of John. I was overjoyed and knew that we were on the same wave-length, which is so important for cospeakers. That all of us should be one had been the dominant theme of my theology for years; John 17 is my favorite Scripture. Adding to my joy at the oneness of this camp was the fact that my interpreter was a Pentecostal minister. She and her husband had been forced out of Cuba by Castro, having been given only one hour to depart. An excellent interpreter as well as person, she suggested that the three of us pray for our unity. A Catholic priest, a Pentecostal minister, and a Protestant laywoman—three nationalities, three denominations, three roles—yet one. I'm sure God's heart was as delighted as mine.

All week long, there had been perfect harmony. The campers were more than hospitable to me. They even thought of me like the Mother Superior of the retreat center where we met. Then came Sunday. My priest-friend Vincent von Euw was to lead mass. He invited the few Protestants to attend. When I inquired about open communion, he said that it was not observed there although he, personally, did not share that opinion. The more intimate I have become with Christ, the more meaningful the sacrament of wine and bread has become. It was a real deprivation for me to attend mass and not receive communion. However, my deep respect for Vincent caused me to accept his invitation despite the fact I didn't know the language or the liturgy and couldn't partake of communion.

Upon entering the sanctuary, I chose a seat on the outside aisle, the least visible as possible. Since I could not participate in the service, for one long hour I pondered the almost life-size form of Christ hanging on the cross. Never before had it been my privilege to meditate upon a crucifix, for as you know, our cross is empty, symbolizing the risen Christ. Never shall I forget that hour, and never shall I be the same. As I gazed upon that face, I felt tears rolling down my cheeks ever so slowly. In a mysterious way, I knew those tears were not mine alone, but his. As my cheeks became damp with his tears, I heard his weeping, and then I heard his words—that he would remain on that cross until we were one and all Christians would commune together. He wept that I was not allowed to participate at his table with my fellow Christians who were Catholic. Jesus and I wept together.

As the service ended, Vincent, who was aware that something was happening to me, came and asked about it. As he held out his arms, I began to sob. Even as I tell this story, I feel the pain of those tears. I told Vincent of my experience, told him what Jesus had said to me. "You must share this with the entire camp," he said. "No, no," I protested. In the camp, there were several Catholic priests as well as a theologian from a seminary in Lima. I was a guest in a foreign land among persons of a different denomination. Yet, when Vincent was halfway through the last talk of the camp, he stopped and said he wanted them to hear what had happened to me. He insisted that I share, and with tears, I did.

The theologian was the first to speak after I had concluded, and naturally, he had to defend his position. However, when he finished his remarks, he approached me, and as he drew closer, I realized there were tears in his eyes, too. Another priest arose and told the campers to always remember what I had said, for it was the most important statement of the entire week. A priest from Chile walked to the microphone. Only twice in his life, he said, had he wept and this was one of those times. I wonder if that special Sunday remains in their memories as it does in mine. It was a history-changing event for some.

The concept of recrucifying Christ had never been in my mind, and I cannot give Scripture reference to defend it. Nevertheless, that day in that little Catholic chapel, I heard Christ weeping over our separation. I have come to believe that our fragmentation—race against race, denomination against denomination, nation against nation—does, indeed, recrucify him.

This has been a sad letter but one I wanted to share with you. It brings us comfort to know that God shares our pain. There is no pain we can ever suffer that Jesus did not endure. The glory is that He has overcome them all. Not that He does not still suffer, but in the end, He is victorious. That is the good news, and that is the meaning of the Gospels: He is risen but yet still being crucified. It is a mystery, but as you ponder the Scriptures, you will come to realize that you must deal with paradox, that which seems contradictory but is essential for the whole truth.

Allen and Virginia, I wish I could spare you from ever having to suffer, but pain and suffering are part of the human condition. Always keep the eternal view, the ultimate victory. Then we can say with Dame Julian of Norwich, "All shall be well, all shall be well, all shall be well."

I love you, dears,
Grandmother

8

Love

Dear Allen and Virginia,

WHAT A SURPRISE, ALLEN, TO SEE YOUR PICTURE ON THE cover of the August 6, 1996, issue of *Time* magazine. It is interesting that they used the same photograph that the *Atlanta Journal* published after the Centennial Olympic Park bombing. How thankful we are that you were not the victim you were shown helping. To me, it seems significant that compassion was your first response, a most necessary attribute in a doctor. I felt it was like God saying, "It is right that Allen is entering medical school within two weeks." So, may you always show that compassion to your patients.

Virginia, I failed to mention in my last letter that I am so thrilled over your semester in Florence, Italy. I am glad that you studied art history in what is perhaps the capital for such a study. Even though that is not your major, it will always bring you an appreciation that otherwise might not have been yours. May you always remember that you are made in the image of God, who is our Creator and who has willed us creative ability.

One of the first verses we learn from the Bible is, "God is love." Not *has* love and doles it out, but *is* love—a very present tense God and a very present love. Never have I doubted God's love, for I was fortunate to have parents who loved me. They didn't talk about love; they lived love. Every unselfish act, every gracious provision, every thoughtful instance of generosity, all said: I love you. I know many persons who have difficulty relating to God as Father, for their earthly fathers were unloving. What an impact our earthly fathers have. Yet, I know that you, as I, have no difficulties in knowing that God is love.

Perhaps the reason that St. John is my favorite gospel writer is because he speaks often of love—God as light, as life, as love. Let me tell you of one way I learned the power of God's love.

After Cliff's death, I needed a job. I applied for and was employed as the first Executive Director of Human Relations for the city of Hopkinsville, Kentucky. As director, I had a weekly radio program. Its purpose was primarily one of education. I interviewed all types: young men still on or just off drugs, white youths as well as black, giving my listeners the opportunity to begin to understand the thinking of young people during the sixties and seventies. When Christmas week came, I changed the format to share with the audience the story of the birth of Christ.

I reread that old familiar story in the Bible. Then, as I meditated upon it before writing my script, I wondered why God chose such an insignificant person and place for this dramatic birth. Why not Jerusalem and a well-known young lady for the mother? As my mind was awhirl with many questions, it finally came to dwell on Mary about whom we know so little. How could she have had such a strange notification from an angel without asking, "Why?" But no, she never asked why she was to be impregnated by the Holy Spirit. She did ask, "How can this be?" But she quickly submitted with, "Let it be, according to your will."

Over and over again I pondered this mystery whose veracity I had at one time doubted. Being chosen by God—

what an amazing thing. Even more amazing were the words that sounded in my heart: "I have chosen another Mary—Mary Virginia." When these startling words were uttered, I was flooded with a love too deep for words.

In that same instant with this overflow of love, there came into my office the most hate-filled person I had ever seen. He was an extremely large black man brimming with anger. I turned from my typewriter, extended my hand, welcomed him, and invited him to be seated and tell me his problem. He did this for one and a half hours. He had just been fired from a job for which he was aptly suited. As he raved about injustices and his dismissal, his anger spewed all over me. Momentarily I thought, why take it out on me? I've never seen this man before. It was obvious that a woman in this position caused his bitterness to increase as did the fact that I was white, and he had just been treated unfairly by a white person.

Just as I began to resent the abusive lanuage hurled at me, God reminded me of the tremendous love he had poured through me. "Give this love to him," I heard. So, I obeyed, letting that overwhelming love flow through me to him. I became fascinated with what was taking place. It seemed that the more love that was channeled toward him the more anger was displayed. Yet, after a period of time, his tone of voice became softer, his language less harsh. Not only was there a change in him, but in me; I began to see him in a new light. My mind began to meditate upon the fact that all that energy could be redirected. I saw potential leadership qualities. As I looked on him with love, he became a new person, a person to whom I could wish a blessed Christmas as he stood up to go. He thanked me for my help. Even though I was not able to settle the initial problem, I realized I had given him a priceless gift: a gift of seeing himself in a new way. Without a word, love had won the battle.

After he left, I considered carefully the divine drama of which I had been one character. "What, God, is the meaning of this?" I asked. The answer I received was that I had participated in a war of hate versus love, and that love had won.

I am thankful that God reminded me of that strange and wonderful experience. Even though I have never since that time experienced such an outflow of love, I know that I can be filled with God's love. I must empty myself to be filled with that same Holy Spirit that enveloped Mary. When the finite and the Infinite meet, when the human and the divine are joined, a new creation comes to birth. "Bring forth, bring forth," I hear the Lord saying to us.

Our world is so filled with injustices. Our world is so filled with angry people. Our world is so filled with the means for destruction from handguns to B-52 bombers. How foolish are we to think that we have to protect ourselves with the same destructive forces used by Satan. God has a higher way, a more excellent way: the way taught by Jesus, the way of love. Not weak human love, but divine love which is always victorious. Glory to the Father and to the Son and to the Holy Spirit. When will we have the faith to try God's way?

In love,
Grandmother

9

The Gift

Dear Allen and Virginia,

THIS MORNING I'M THINKING ABOUT WHAT COMES FIRST: giving or receiving. God answered this question for me dramatically a few years ago.

Miss Estelle Carver, the great Bible teacher of whom I have spoken, had been in Hopkinsville, Kentucky, for a week. She had been invited by Church Women United to lead a school of prayer. I was doubly blessed, for she stayed in my home and occupied the "prophet's chamber," as she called the upstairs bedroom. Each night as she slowly climbed the stairs (she had just turned eighty but assured me that Moses just started out when he was eighty), she always quoted words of St. Francis. Each morning, she called down the stairs, "This is the day the Lord has made," to which I was expected to respond, "Let us rejoice and be glad in it." Her whole life was filled with life-giving words. Needless to say, a week with Estelle left one on a spiritual high, although she would never have used such terminology, the correct English woman that she was.

Dr. James Robertson, a United Methodist minister, gave a series of sermons at a Methodist church shortly after Estelle left, so those of us who were spiritually hungry were fed rich food. It was in such a condition that I started out alone to a speaking engagement in Owensboro, Kentucky.

I was so filled with unspeakable joy that my whole being was focused on the Lord. A picture (some would call it a vision) was given to me. I found myself before a large, marble altar, and behind the altar was God. My soul yearned to offer a gift, yet what? I recall racking my brain to think what I could give this God who was so good. The only things I could think of were my ability to organize and my experience in speaking. I stood there, so small in comparison to this majestic God. Timidly, I lifted my hands with these two gifts. As I made the gesture, a giant hand swung down and slapped my gifts from me. I heard the words, "I don't want your gifts."

If you've never stood naked before the Lord without one thing to give, you can't know the shame, the awful agony I experienced. Tears began to roll down my cheeks with a sorrow such as I had never known. Remember, my children, I'm driving alone to a neighboring town on one of Kentucky's many toll roads, and I went right through one of the toll gates. This set the sirens sounding and alerted the security guards. I hastened to back up and attempted to pay the toll. With tears still rolling down my cheeks, I searched and fumbled in my purse for the necessary fifty cents, no doubt convincing the attendant that women should never be given driving permits.

After meeting the law's requirements, I started out again still emotionally shattered. Once more I was directed to look upon that huge marble altar. As I looked, the table was no longer empty. On it was the form of Christ. Startled at the change, I heard a firm yet loving voice: "Look. Christ is the gift. Christ has done it all. It is finished. Receive, receive."

Those words were loud and clear . . . receive, receive. How topsy-turvy was my theology. I thought I was the doer. I had to work; I had to give. With determination and stubborn persistency, I had worked when all the time the work was finished. He, Jesus, had done it all. Receive, receive.

A different person stood up to speak to that congregation on the subject of prayer. My whole understanding had to be revised on the basis of this revelation. How humbling. May you, my dear ones, learn first to receive.

Grandmother

10

Strength

Dear Allen and Virginia,

THROUGH THE YEARS, I HAVE LEARNED THAT REGARDLESS of the number of disclosures, God is so much bigger, so much more majestic, and so much more loving than my earlier concepts. It is thrilling to know that this great God—this universal Lover—is personal and is eager to open the eyes of our hearts to see more and more.

As you will discern from these letters, my spiritual journey is mostly one of correcting errors of false theology. Having at one time thought of God as only resting, today I want to tell you about a time when I learned differently.

My sisters Dorothy and Christine met me in Guam when I was visiting you and your family, Allen. (Virginia, you were not yet on the scene.) After spending a few days with your family, the three of us went to Japan where we joined a tour traveling to Hong Kong and Thailand. After a most fascinating sightseeing adventure, we returned to Tokyo where we caught a plane for home. It was very disconcerting to leave Tokyo on the evening of March 4 and arrive in Honolulu in the early morning hours of March 4. Flying into the Honolulu airport was spectacular. Looking down on the whole world covered with fluffy white clouds through which the early sunlight was beginning to peek, I knew that I was seeing the world as it must have been on the very first day of creation. It was a scene I shall never forget.

When checking in at the airport, the agent in charge asked if we would mind sitting in first class. Naturally, we wouldn't! After that long flight, we dreamed of resting. Dorothy and Christine were seated together; I was moved three times until I had a window seat on the left. As I was about to settle down for a nap, the agent who had asked me to move came on board supporting a half-drunken man who was cursing and causing much disturbance. He was literally poured into the seat next to me, all the while demanding another drink. Disheveled, drunk, cursing, and smelling foul, in slurred speech he said, "You've got me for a seatmate all the way to Los Angeles." "So I see," I replied. Then I looked into his agonized face.

At one time his general condition would have so disgusted me, I would not have acknowledged his presence. But I turned to him and said, "What is your problem?" Then, he poured out his grief, all the time cursing God and requesting another drink. The story he blurted out was that he had just learned that one of his five-year-old twin boys had drowned that morning in Los Angeles. The man who brought him on the plane was the boy's godfather. In sympathy, this person had said, "I know how you feel." This increased Chip's (I later learned his name) anger, and he shouted at me, "He doesn't know how I feel. He's never had a son to die." "But I have," I said. A bond was created.

Chip explained his appearance by telling me that he was in the midst of painting his house, preparing it for sale. He and his family were moving to Los Angeles. Chip's shouting and cursing were interrupted occasionally by his telling me bits about himself. He was in the banking business in Honolulu, but as a young man, he had gone to seminary after college with the view of becoming a minister. However, he suffered a great disillusionment in seminary from which he never recovered. His faith in God was shattered.

So, he blamed God for the drowning of his son. His anger was so great that once he asked me if I knew what would happen if he ran his fist through the window on my side. I said I didn't know, but I was under the impression that I would be sucked out and, possibly, he would be, too. As he beat his fists against the seat in front of us, he said he could not get off the plane in Los Angeles. He would not; he could not face his wife.

Now and then he would bring up a current topic, and we would have a few moments of conversation. It was rather strange (or was it?) how many interests we had in common. Then, he would return to the raging oaths and threats. Each time he went to the restroom, I feared for his life since he certainly seemed suicidal.

About an hour out of Los Angeles, I turned to Chip and said, "Chip, I have listened to you all across the Pacific. Now, you are going to listen to me." I grabbed his left hand in both of my hands. "You do not believe in God," I told him, "but I do. You do not believe in prayer, but I do. Now you are going to listen to me pray." Suddenly, he became still. "I am going to pray that God gives you an inner strength to face your wife who not only is grieving as you are but no doubt feels guilty for not having watched your son more closely."

Let me confess, dear children, I never prayed so hard. With passion, I beseeched God to give Chip the needed courage to face his wife and the sorrow which was theirs. Touch his distraught heart, oh Lord, and let him know your presence. Later, after my prayer, Chip stood up and went to the restroom where he washed his face and combed his hair. When he returned, he looked sober. It had been arranged that he would be the first one off the plane when we landed. As I saw him straighten his shoulders and walk to meet his father-in-law, I had a great sense that my prayer had been answered.

God was at work. God was giving Chip a strength that he did not believe possible. As for me, I rejoiced to see that God engineers these circumstances. Perhaps I was the only person on that plane who could identify with his sorrow, his anger, his questioning. Perhaps I was the only one who needed to see God at work, arranging where I sat so I could be available for one of God's needy sons. It is good to know that God is not retired as I once thought, depending on each of us to be solely responsible for carrying out divine work. Never are we working alone. Never are we suffering alone. Never are we limited to our own weaknesses. God's strength is always available. What a wonderful God whom we can call Father.

God bless Chip, wherever he is. God bless you two wonderful grandchildren whom I love very much.

Grandmother

11

Oneness

Dear Allen and Virginia,

THIS MORNING I WANT TO WRITE ABOUT WHAT THOMAS Kelly calls "living life from the center." I do hope you will come to treasure Thomas Kelly's *Testament of Devotion* as much as I do. Aside from the Bible, that little book of less than one hundred pages has challenged, inspired, and enlightened me more than perhaps any other one book. I bought my first copy in 1955 at my first Camp Farthest Out. Thankfully, it is now being reprinted with an introduction by Douglas Steere and accompanied by comments from Richard Foster, author of *Celebration of Discipline.*

Thomas Kelly was a Quaker whose book is a series of devotional essays gathered, as Steere says, "without the critical revision that the author might have given them had he lived." *Testament of Devotion* is considered a spiritual classic, and for me, the thrill of it is the way in which Kelly not only lets the reader in on the secret life of Jesus, but also opens the door for everyone who would follow.

When I first read Kelly, my imagination was captured. I didn't pretend to understand much of what I read, but it stirred within me a tremendous desire to know the truth of which he spoke. As I read and reread,

I yearned to understand and digest his insights of living life from the center. He speaks of inward worship and listening as being the heart of religion:

> It is the secret, I am persuaded of the inner life of the Master of Galilee. He expected this secret to be freshly discovered in everyone who would be his follower. It creates an amazing fellowship, the church catholic and invisible, and institutes group living at a new level, a society grounded in reverence, history rooted in eternity, colonies of heaven.

St. Paul's letter to the Colossians opened new dimensions in my understanding of living life from the center. In the graphic portrait of Jesus in the first chapter, Paul, in the seventeenth verse, makes the startling statement, "In union with God all things find their proper place" (GNB). As one who had spent years trying to get the inner and the outer together, that statement exploded in my mind. Fragmented by many selves, each competing for my time and attention, I suffered frustration. Wanting to be the perfect homemaker, wife, mother, and civic and religious leader, I longed for a life integrated and whole. Being in union with God was the solution.

A fourteenth-century writer, Dame Julian of Norwich, well known through her book *Revelation of Divine Love*, coined a word that I find very expressive: the word is *oned*. To be *oned with God* then all things have their proper place. Another unique expression of hers is the statement, "Betwixt God and me, there is no between."

As an explosive light went on in my mind regarding this union or *onedness*, God gave me a picture of my life as He designed it to be. Instead of the scatteredness of my many selves, I saw a circle with Christ at the center from which all facets of my life radiated. With this picture and the prompting by the Spirit that I was to live from that center who is Christ, I inwardly shouted, "It all makes sense!"

What a simplification of life this centering brings: no longer listening to many voices, but One Voice; no longer panting feverishly; no longer having to respond to all requests but only those to which Christ calls me. Immediately I recognized that I had to learn to say no. What a terribly hard job for one who is accustomed to responding to every need. I had to learn that the need is not the call. Through the years, it has become evident that if I heed that One Voice, God gives me energy to fulfill the requests. If I listen only to that Voice and pay little or no attention to the ones who do not understand why their requests go unheeded, life from the Center brings simplification.

Gradually, we get the message: one Lord, one Master with whom we must be in constant communion. Kelly concludes *Testament of Devotion* with the following passage:

> Life from the Center is a life of unhurried peace and power. It is simple. It is serene. It is amazing. It is triumphant. It is radiant. It takes no time, but it occupies all our time. And it makes our life programs new and overcoming. We need not get frantic. He is at the helm. And when our little day is done we lie down quietly in peace, for all is well.

That is the life of a disciple. Living life from the center is my call. This I know.

Lovingly,
Grandmother

communion

Good morning, Virginia and Allen,

WE ARE TOLD IN 1 JOHN THAT WE LOVE BECAUSE GOD first loved us (4:19). Love is the key message of Jesus. He saw the interconnectedness between love of God and love of self and neighbor when he took the words from Deuteronomy 6:4 about loving God and Leviticus 14:18 about loving neighbor and joined them in the Great Commandment. They are no longer separate, but one.

Love is the message of God who is love. A great teacher of the early church, Bernard of Clairvaux (1090–1153), wrote a treatise which lists four degrees of love:

1. Love self for self's sake;
2. Love God for self's sake;
3. Love God for God's sake; and
4. Love self for God's sake.

Our spiritual life starts much like our physical life. A baby is pampered and made the center of the universe, as that baby loves self for self alone. Then, in our spiritual walk, the second degree is exhibited: we love God for what we can get from that relationship. Growth through prayer and spiritual discipline bring us to a degree of loving God for God's sake. Our intimacy has developed to the point of enjoyment and comfort in the presence of God; communion takes place. Bernard's fourth degree of loving self for God's sake is rare. When a person has come to his or her "true self," of which Thomas Merton wrote "the self designed by God," then oneness takes place.

We hear from theologians, psychiatrists, psychologists, and social workers that to love and be loved are the most important things to a person's mental, emotional, and spiritual health. The interconnectedness of body, mind, and spirit has long interested me. My only brother, Ben, developed a severe form of asthma at six months of age. My parents followed every lead they could which might cure or at least benefit him. But all to no avail. Then I began to read of the connection between anxiety in the mother and the attack of asthma in the child. This started my interest in the effects of the psychic on the physical.

For years I have known that we can literally make ourselves sick. Yet, can we reverse that? Once in the hospital after a heart attack, I found that the surrender of my will to God and the repetition of Scripture that was given to me—"In returning and rest shall you be saved; in quietness and confidence shall be your strength" (Is. 30:15)—could quiet my body until my blood pressure was lowered. This was long before the general public knew about biofeedback. (I was glad that I did not know the conclusion of that verse: "And you would not.") It seems that our society is slow to learn that which the Scriptures have taught us all along—the connectedness, the interconnectedness, God and man, man to man.

Long before I understood the meaning of the oneness for which Jesus prayed in John 17, it appealed to me in such a way that I even wrote a religious drama for my church's one hundred twenty-fifth anniversary entitled *That They May All Be One*. As an activitist, I tried to make us one—alike, dittoes. But that was not it. Then I thought it meant oneness with God, like the relationship between Jesus and his Father, God. For a period, I dwelt on the oneness within my many selves. However, it encompasses all three: oneness with self, oneness with others, and oneness with God. For my present understanding, the oneness between self and God must come first.

God is the initiator, the designer. Harmony among people must exist if we are to live in the Kingdom Jesus proclaimed. The Kingdom is here now. I truly believe that I, as an individual, cannot be the person I am designed to be until you, also, become who and what you were created to be. In Hebrews 11:39–40, we read, "And all these, though well attested by their faith, did not receive what was promised, since God had foreseen something better for us, that apart from us they should not be made perfect."

Individualism has played havoc with relationships. Relationships must be examined. While working in the area of human relations, I found myself giving workshops on prayer one weekend, for that was my primary interest, and on the next weekend, a seminar on human relations. For a time, I kept them separate, but the longer I heard the heart cries of persons to whom we churchgoers had been unjust, the clearer I saw the gap which separated one group from the next. My awareness of the need for interconnectedness between relationship to God and relationship to all human beings grew stronger.

God's commandment to love is the key. Oh, may we learn to live love.

Shalom,
Grandmother

Peace

Dear Allen and Virginia,

"WHERE DID YOU GET THAT PEACE?" WAS THE QUESTION a young doctor asked me. But before I tell you my answer or lack of an answer, let me start at the beginning.

Jesus asks of us the impossible. Only those who have tried to follow his lead know how traumatic it is. To try to do something for which you do not have the ability leads only to frustration. Then we read St. Augustine's words: Jesus became human that we humans might become divine.

Often our thinking is that God will do a patch-up job on us, and then we can obey. Yet, that is not according to the plan. God does not want to put a clean coat on us to cover a dirty body but wants to make us brand new from the inside out. Jesus came in order to be the regenerator; he puts in us his heredity. St. Paul spoke of his own travails "until Christ is formed in you" (Gal. 4:19). Almost daily I pray the following prayer by Bishop Carey:

> O holy Spirit of God, come into my heart
>   and fill me.
> I open wide all the windows of my soul to
>   let thee in.

Come and possess me completely.
I offer thee the only thing I really possess,
My capacity to be filled with thee and by
    thee.
Of myself, I am an unprofitable servant,
An empty vessel to be used, to be filled,
To be consecrated for thy service.

Fill me, so that I may live the life of thy
    spirit
The life of truth and goodness;
    the life of beauty, love and joy,
    the life of wisdom and strength.

Guide me today in all things,
Guide me to the people I should meet or
    help.
Guide me to the circumstances in which I
    can best serve you.
But above all, make Christ to be formed in
    me
That I may dethrone self in the heart
And crown him king.

Bind and cement Christ to me by all thy
    ways
    known and unknown;
By holy thoughts, by unseen graces,
By sacramental ties
So that I abide in you and you abide in me
Today and forever. Amen.

The key is: God provides. The old must go; the new
heart, the new life must come.

    Now, back to the initial question: "Where did you get
that peace?" It happened in this way. While I was still

living in Hopkinsville, Kentucky, I was sent to St. Thomas Hospital in Nashville, Tennessee, with an apparent heart attack. The tests I underwent included an arteriogram, and several doctors assisted in this procedure. The primary doctor on my right said that I could watch on the monitor over my shoulder if I wished. It was my wish, for I thought I might as well get my money's worth. As I watched that tiny tube work its way up my body from the groin into my heart, I was fascinated by what I observed. Then dye was inserted into the tube, and I saw no more. I knew no more.

"Wake up! Wake up! Mrs. Parrish, Mrs. Parrish," the doctor on my right called out. The young medic on the left bent over me and asked, almost hungrily: "Mrs. Parrish, where did you get that peace?" Even as he asked, I was aware that a floodgate had opened and through me poured a peace which defied understanding. I had nothing to do with this peace. I did not create it; I did not generate it. It was simply as though I were connected to a huge reservoir and through me was transmitted this powerful peace.

About this time, the primary doctor said, "Mrs. Parrish, your chest will be quite sore for days. Your heart stopped, and we had to use extreme shock to make it start again." Sure enough, there were marks on my chest in the form of circles which lasted for a number of days. Somehow, I secretly wished those imprints would have remained, for they spoke of the crown of thorns Jesus wore for me.

Such an unusual happening must be reflected upon. What was the meaning? I have learned that everything is significant, that nothing happens outside the will of God. So, a few days later I spoke to the Lord about the river of peace that had flooded that hospital room. "Lord," I asked, "must I really *die* before your peace will come through me?"

"Mary Virginia," the reply came. "You are finally getting the message. The old self must die. Without death, there is no resurrection. You must die so that I, the great I AM, may live in you. This is why Jesus' death must be received as your death so that his resurrected life can be yours. Take. Receive."

God asks of us the impossible, but the God I've come to know provides all we need. Jesus is Lord of the impossible. The Holy Spirit is given that we might have that same life which Jesus had. That is the way—the only way we can become like Christ. C. S. Lewis daringly wrote that we were to become little Christs. Such transformation is our goal. May that goal become yours.

With love,
Grandmother

simplicity

Dear Allen and Virginia,

GREETINGS FROM YOUR GRANDMOTHER WHO LOVES YOU very much. Even more important is the fact that God loves you with an unconditional love. That is truly awesome. Do you realize that you can do nothing that makes God love you less nor anything that will make God love you more? Jesus demonstrated the extent of that love from the cross. Then, after his resurrection, he gave the Holy Spirit that we might do the works that he did.

I guess I have always believed that Jesus was to be our pattern. It was only after futile attempts to copy him that I realized I needed more than a pattern. I needed empowerment. As I've written, I needed the Holy Spirit. Only after much searching and much prayer, I have some understanding of this need and how it is met. Not having had original sin impressed upon me from the pulpit, sin was not a problem. It took personal experience and observation for me to realize how very self-centered human beings are. We need to be changed to Christ-centeredness, and this change requires the working of the Holy Spirit.

"Jesus Loves Me" was the first song I ever learned. It fulfilled all my needs. But, like many others, my childish concept of Jesus changed, and I thought more of God the Invisible who seemed remote. Like Adam, I could run and hide when disobedient. Many people seem content to keep their childish beliefs without questioning. Sometimes I almost envy those who are satisfied to accept what others say we should believe. That has never been my experience.

To grow from childishness to childlikeness takes many years; at least it did for me. I feel somewhat like Malcolm Muggeridge who rediscovered Jesus, an experience he describes in his book *Jesus Rediscovered*. Only then could I begin to know and see the role of Mary, the mother of Jesus, in this holy drama. The finite and Infinite join, and a new creature is brought forth. Praise God, if we seek long enough and persistently enough, we will be brought to that awareness which is simplicity of faith. Karl Barth, the Swiss theologian, upon leaving the United States after a visit here was asked by news reporters, "Of all your vast theological knowledge, what truth do you consider to be the greatest?" To the consternation of the newspersons, he answered, "Jesus loves me this I know, for the Bible tells me so."

Who is this Jesus, the God-man? I love Paul's description of him in Colossians, even though all Scripture reveals his nature when we have eyes to see and hearts to accept. Let us examine what Jesus says about himself. Jesus knew where He had come from, where He was going, and He is eager to show us the Way. People of all ages are leaving families, quitting jobs, and searching in all sorts of places trying to "find themselves." Our society today is composed of many on such a search. Jesus' words regarding who He is answers my longtime quest. Jesus said:

> I AM THE LIGHT OF THE WORLD
> are you in darkness?
> I AM THE LIVING BREAD
> are you hungry?
> I AM THE DOOR
> I'll give you the key.
> I AM THE GOOD SHEPHERD

let me protect you.
I AM THE VINE
stay connected to me.
I AM THE RESURRECTION AND THE LIFE
you, too, can live in a higher dimension.
I AM THE WAY, THE TRUTH
will you follow me?
I AM THE SON OF GOD
you, too, are a child of God.

When we truly accept this God-man Jesus, this Lord of all, our minds are opened to the magnificent truth that God wants all of us to have as close a relationship with him as Jesus had. Too wonderful to believe? Dare we risk it?

Relationship is what the Christian life is all about. We are given only two commandments: love God with our entire being and love our neighbors as ourselves. Many say to me, I can love my neighbor, but I can't love myself. I can forgive my neighbor, but I can't forgive myself.

Loving oneself is essential to loving one's neighbor—not in a self-centered way, but a Christ-centered way. God's plan is for us to be like Jesus, while retaining our individual uniqueness, for God makes no carbon copies. St. Augustine wrote that God made us for himself and that our souls are restless till they find rest in him. This is truth. In finding God, we find ourselves.

My dear grandchildren, I pray you find God's rest.

Agape,
Grandmother

15

Healing

Dear Allen and Virginia,

IN JOHN 14:12 JESUS IS QUOTED AS SAYING, "HE WHO believes in me will also do the works that I do . . ." Don't I believe in him? Yet, where are the works—the preaching, the teaching, the healing? This third act of Jesus, healing, seems to hold a fascination for us all. We are drawn to the dramatic, the unusual, and the unexplained.

It was a revelation to hear at a seminar on healing that anyone who had received a healing was more apt to be so gifted. That caught my attention. Had I not been a recipient of healing when your mother was in my womb? But surely not me, I thought.

God moves quickly once our attention is caught. On returning home from the Camp Farthest Out where I had attended the seminar, I found your mom had come home from Brownie Scout camp with a horrible case of poison ivy. Her face was so swollen she was unrecognizable. Her eyes were shut tight.

The following morning when I came up the stairs from my little prayer room, the words "lay your hands on Ann Carter's eyes" came to me. Entering into this conversation, I said, "Surely Lord, you don't mean me. I can't heal anyone." My doubts were met with his response: "I didn't tell you to heal her. I know you can't heal, but I can. I repeat, lay your hands on her eyes."

Dare I? What should I say? To perform such an act was frightening to me, but without a word, I obeyed, actually laying my hands upon her. "Are you praying?" she asked. Somewhat embarrassed in my first attempt to pray for healing, I confessed, "Yes."

A short time later my husband called to remind me to take Ann Carter to the pediatrician for her second in a series of shots for such a severe case of poison ivy. "Tell Daddy I don't need to go," she prompted. I forget his response, but she did not go, and within two days, she was completely healed.

Her faith? My obedience? A natural phenomenon? These questions flooded my mind, but I could not argue with the reality of this unusual happening.

After this experience, I was instructed by God's inner voice to go to a friend and pray for her healing. This I did, and healing was hers. Then came a time when our prayer group prayed for days and months for a young man, and nothing happened. No physical healing occurred, but possibly a more important thing happened: a spiritual, psychological healing that made an impact on his family.

Only when I've been nudged by God have I continued praying for physical healings. I've come to believe that all ills, all restlessness, and all diseases are of spiritual origin. My prayers have to start with a person's or a group's relationship with God.

My desire for healing among races prompted me to accept the position of director for the Commission on Human Relations in Hopkinsville. It was with reluctance that I agreed to the assignment, but I believed it to be the will of God. I knew it would involve pain . . . how much, I had no idea. During those seven years in city hall, my heart was broken not only by rejection but also by hearing stories of injustices day after day after day.

On the door of my office, I placed a poster with the words: "Together, let us make this a city under God." Below these words a white hand was shown clasping a black hand. So strong was my desire for reconciliation among races that I felt as if I were partly responsible for the murder of Dr. Martin Luther King Jr. In my journal I wrote a litany of confession (which was later used at an ecumenical service) seeking God's forgiveness.

Various opportunities for short-term missions in developing countries have made me realize more keenly the necessity of being healed of prejudice. The cultural belief that being white, American, and Protestant makes one superior must be eradicated. Inbred prejudice must be recognized and healing must take place if races are ever to live together in harmony and peace.

Healing among denominations has always had a major place in my prayers. While in London, I recall visiting a small chapel in Westminster Abbey then promptly going to Westminster Cathedral where I prayed for healing between Protestants and Catholics. After kneeling in prayer in the small chapel dedicated to unity among people, I started to leave but was then compelled to return and light a candle. A simple act, but one that has influenced my life significantly.

May we learn to appreciate our diversity. May intolerance give way to "seeing" all persons as Jesus did, all one under God. Jesus broke down the walls which separate us. May our every act, our every word, our every thought build bridges among races, among denominations, among nations.

Healing, whether physical, psychological, or spiritual, needs to take place among nations, and it starts with you and me. You, my grandchildren, will live out your lives in a world that needs people who have received love and are willing to give the unconditional, grace-filled love of God. Such love heals. Receive God's love, and give it.

I love you,
Grandmother

Discipleship

Dear Allen and Virginia,

THIS MORNING, LET'S THINK TOGETHER ABOUT DISCIPLESHIP. Just now, I've been reading about Jesus selecting the twelve disciples, ordinary fishermen. Not a single one was highly educated; not a single one possessed any awards for achievements. Just folks. They bring to mind words that my friend Mary Webster once spoke to me. I had been invited to lead a school of prayer and had become acutely aware of my inadequacy to fulfill this task. How could I who knew so little about prayer speak on such a sacred theme? How dare I attempt to assuage the hunger of people's hearts for the living Bread of Life? After I confessed my fears, Mary said, "Don't be afraid, Mary Virginia. God's desperate. God will use anybody."

No truer words were ever spoken. It is not the most brilliant that God uses. It is the most available, the most trusting, and the most faithful. That description *can* include you and me.

For years, I had confused church membership with discipleship. We become very excited over someone's conversion and rightly so. However, we often stop there. We fail to take the newly born through the long, tedious process of growth. John the Baptist *grew*. Jesus *grew* in wisdom and stature and in favor with God and man. We are instructed by Jesus, by Paul, and by Peter to GROW UP. Discipleship involves growth.

From Dietrich Bonhoeffer, we learned the cost of discipleship in his book by that title. Now, according to Dallas Willard in *The Spirit of the Disciplines*, non-discipleship robs us of:

1. Abiding peace.
2. A life penetrated throughout by love.
3. A faith that sees everything in the light of God's overriding governance for good.
4. A hopefulness that stands firm in the most discouraging of circumstances.
5. A power to do what is right and withstand the forces of evil.
6. The abundant life Jesus came to give.

With such a loss, aren't we willing to become disciplined disciples?

Most of us, according to Evelyn Underhill, spend our lives conjugating the three verbs: to *want*, to *have*, and to *do*, rather than dealing with the fundamental verb, to *be*. Just *being* seems such a waste of time. As a natural-born doer, this is a hard lesson. We even carry into our spiritual journeys these same clutching, grabbing, restless attitudes of the activist. Hurrying to all the spiritual meetings, wanting to read all the spiritual books, desiring to meet all the spiritual leaders, we become spiritual gluttons. We still have not gotten the message—the supreme fact that God is the *doer* and *being* is our work.

Learning to BE requires that we
>   Be present,
>   Be aware,
>   Be holy (compassionate).

On being present:

> To *God* . . . Learning God's language.
>
> To *self* . . . What are you cramming into your mind? Are you listening to your body (a lesson I'm beginning to learn)? Are you present to your pain? Your sorrows? Or, are you trying to stifle them through much busyness, many activities? Be present to them.
>
> To *others* . . . One of the greatest gifts we can give to another is to listen with our whole being. We do not have to solve the problem. We do not have to fix the situation. We only have to *be there*.

On being aware:

> To be aware of life, all senses attuned to the moment—the smell of it, the sight of it, the taste of it, and the sound of it. We are reprimanded by Jesus to *see*, to *hear*, to *taste*.

On being holy:

> One translation uses the word *compassionate* instead of holy. If we live with *passion*, it means we are fully alive, fully aware, and fully responsive to God, to self, to others. Therein lies holiness.

When we accept the invitation of Jesus to be a disciple, he invites us to *come* to him, *walk* with him, *work* with him, and *watch* with him.

Walking holds no special charm for me. If I could jog, that might seem like fun. If I could run against the wind and reach that "high" runners are supposed to reach, that would be exhilarating. But walking, just walking, is such a humdrum pursuit.

I recall one of the first young women who came to me for spiritual direction over a period of time. One day, she was so relieved when I expressed the fact that, at times, keeping up a devotional period could be so dreary, such plain drudgery. She had assumed that every day was a mountaintop experience for me. Her relief taught me to share not only the glorious times with the Lord, but the monotonous times of daily appointments: the same time, the same place, the same Scripture (I have learned to vary it). However, without these daily, deadly times, there would be no high moments of enlightenment and glory. Without these disciplines, when it seems nothing is happening, when standing before the Lord seems so futile, disciples would never know the intimacy of disclosure as to who Jesus really is—of knowing God.

My favorite picture of Jesus as a youth is that of his working beside his earthly father, Joseph. How intent he appears in watching, how eager to learn the way to make the finest yoke. As he worked and watched, we also need to work and watch God. Then we are not so apt to become bored and discouraged. But if we do, Eugene Peterson has a word for us in *The Message*:

> Are you tired? Worn out? Burned out on religion? Come to me. Get away with me and you'll recover your life. I'll show you how to do it. Learn the unforced rhythms of grace. I won't lay anything heavy or ill fitting on you. Keep company with me and you'll learn to live freely and lightly (Matt. 11:28–30).

Who can refuse such an offer?

Lovingly,
Grandmother

Messages

Dear Allen and Virginia,

THIS MORNING I WANT TO SHARE WITH YOU A DIFFERENT way in which God speaks. Variety seems to be very much a part of God's nature. I recall my trip to Australia as one of such discovery. So many different animals I had never seen before. So much plant life that was totally new to us Americans. What an amazing world God created.

Once at a meeting, I felt a hand on my shoulder, and words were spoken by the person behind me: "God is telling me that you are the one to replace me when I retire." I neither knew the person who spoke nor could I quickly accept her message as God-sent. Since her work dealt with prayer and the spiritual life had become my primary interest, I was somewhat puzzled. I hastened to inquire of Glenn Harding, a mature Christian friend of mine: "What must I think? Does God speak in such a way?" Glenn gave me sound advice. He said I should not take her word as final. Even so, I should be open to the possibility. I should pray and only respond when God confirmed it to me.

For five months I sought the will of God regarding this position. I never attained inner assurance that it was the correct path for me. To the committee in search of a replacement, I answered, "No." Later on, circumstances definitely confirmed that my answer was in accordance with God's will.

It was some twenty years later that a second person approached me with such a *message* from God. The scene was a Camp Farthest Out in New York where I was a speaker. The *messenger* was a member of the prayer group to which I was assigned. With a great sense of humility Evie Day said, "Mary Virginia, God is telling me that you are to stop speaking all over the world [as I had been doing for the previous fifteen years] and that you are to train young women in prayer and the spiritual life." I told her I would pray about it and see if my guidance confirmed hers.

I remembered Glenn's counsel that God should speak to me in a definite way. There was an immediate resistance in me to stop public speaking. This I loved. Not only was it a wonderful travel experience, but it fed my ego, I had to confess to myself. There is a great thrill in having an audience of fifty to five hundred persons listening with encouragement and support. Something happens between speaker and audience which is electric. If I followed the direction of training a few women, it would hinder my time allowed for speaking engagements. Nevertheless, I could not ignore the prophetic word. I had to be willing. It came gradually that the word spoken to me might be the will of God. I had grown to appreciate those who were definitely interested in things of the Spirit and who might be willing to commit themselves to a disciplined life of prayer.

How to proceed? I called together three young women who had come to me at various times for spiritual counsel. I knew their love for me and their sincere love of Jesus. I told them what I was thinking and wanted to know if they would be interested in committing themselves for two years to such a plan. I had an inner certainty that it was only the deeply committed who would be interested in such a disciplined life. When their answer came as a positive "yes" asking if I would teach them if they were the only ones interested, I knew that God was calling me to this ministry.

Since the three lived in different towns and even in different states, I would not limit my invitations to persons from Kentucky. We agreed that our meetings should be in a place where silence and solitude were possible. The Catherine Spaulding Center at Nazareth, Kentucky, run by the Sisters of Charity was selected, for it met the criteria.

What would be the minimum discipline, Lord? We planned to have twice-a-year retreats of four days at which time not only would there be teaching on spiritual formation and the spiritual disciplines, but exercises to be done alone and in small groups. Private conferences with each member would be held. Disciplines for daily devotional periods at home would be agreed upon by those called.

Dates were set for retreats for two years, and invitations were sent to about eighteen women. Several responded with interest but couldn't commit. Eleven women met at Nazareth, Kentucky, for the first retreat in 1989. They came from five different states and five different Protestant denominations. Could such a diverse group ever become a community? The one thing we had in common was hunger, a hunger to have an intimate relationship with the living Lord and a willingness to start on a spiritual journey.

It was agreed that we should have a name, but what? After much prayer, it was proposed: The Other Marys. In a New Testament translation, it states that at the tomb of Jesus there was Mary his mother, Mary Magdalene, and the other Mary. Since we wanted to follow in such a train, this seemed appropriate. We sometimes had to do a lot of explaining to the Sisters and their guests at Nazareth regarding our name!

As of 1997, The Other Marys have recommitted themselves every two years and are entering their ninth year. The group has become smaller, for one member died, another had to resign shortly after we started, and a third did not recommit herself after the first two years, because God was calling her in a different direction. From this group of seven plus me, other groups have been born, but I will tell you of them in my next letter. In retrospect, I am sure that Evie Day was speaking for God that day.

Bless you, my dears. My prayers are always with you, especially at your exam time.

Grandmother

Listening

Dear Allen and Virginia,

I'LL BRING YOU UP TO DATE ON WHAT KEEPS ME BUSY. IN my last letter, I told you about The Other Marys. Now, I'll tell you about the two additional groups I lead in spiritual formation.

Right here, let me offer you the best definition of spiritual formation I know. In his *Workbook on Living Prayer*, Maxie Dunnam, who is the current president of Asbury Theological Seminary, wrote:

> Spiritual formation is that dynamic process of receiving through faith and appropriating through commitment, discipline and action, the living Christ into our own life to the end that our life will conform to and manifest the reality of Christ's presence in the world.

This is quite an order: to conform to and manifest Christ's presence in the world. Yet, that is why Jesus came, to show us what a real child of God looks like, then to send the Holy Spirit to indwell and make possible more and more children of God. We're all children, but true children (ones who know who they are) can, as Maxie Dunnam says, live that Christ-styled life.

On learning of my ministry among The Other Marys, Dr. James Long, senior pastor of Atlanta's North Avenue Presbyterian Church, where I am a member, asked if I would lead such a group at North Avenue, and moreover, would I be willing to include men. "Yes," I answered to both questions, "if they are willing to commit themselves for two years and are willing to follow the daily disciplines." "Then, let me be the first to sign up," said Jim, and he was. Sadly, he became terminally ill and was unable to participate, but he gave his enthusiastic endorsement and great encouragement to proceed.

After agreeing to take on another group, I was overwhelmed with a great sense of inadequacy and cried out, "Help me, Lord." Three doors were opened to equip me for this ministry. Dr. Ben Campbell Johnson invited me to audit his courses on spirituality at Columbia Seminary. Fr. Niel Jarreau, a Jesuit, was willing to take me through the *Spiritual Exercises of St. Ignatius* over a period of months. Then, I was able to attend a weekend retreat on centering prayer conducted by Fr. Thomas Keating, a Trappist monk. These opportunities for equipping myself were coming so rapidly, I had to call out, "Enough, Lord!" The original D and D group, which means Discipline and Discovery (since men were now involved, The Other Marys seemed inappropriate), is now in its sixth year, the members recommitting themselves every two years.

After the first two years, the minister of discipleship at North Avenue asked if I would lead another group. "Yes," I answered, "if they are willing to abide by the same requirements." Twelve responded that they would like to become so disciplined. Two were unable to sign up for the second two-year term, so now there are ten who are starting their third year.

As I think of the many changes in my life after the age of seventy, I am so glad that I moved to Atlanta in 1985 to be near you and your family. God has opened a much broader ministry. God always knows best. It is we who drag our feet and either do not see God's will or openly refuse to obey it.

The private conferences which I have with each individual have no doubt provided the greatest opportunity for me to grow in the dimension of prayer. Listening is a discipline which takes on greater importance all the time. Hence, I love the following words of Douglas Steere, a saintly Quaker: "To 'listen' another's soul into a condition of disclosure and discovery may be almost the greatest service that any human being ever performs for another."

In *Testament of Devotion*, Thomas Kelly introduced me to the idea of listening on two levels at once. Such a possibility of listening to God while listening to a person fascinated me and became a goal of mine. I have discovered the joy of this dual listening; it brings a level of discernment far beyond a person's own listening skill.

That's what makes this spiritual life so exciting. There are always new things to learn, new skills to acquire. Let me urge you two to never stop learning.

Love,
Grandmother

Disciplines

Dear Virginia,

I ADDRESS THIS LETTER TO YOU, FOR YOU WERE THE ONE who asked, "Grandmommy, were you scared?" The question came two weeks after I had been rushed to the emergency room with congestive heart failure. I was thankful to be able to answer honestly, "No, Virginia, I wasn't scared. I knew my condition was serious. I realized I could die, but I was not afraid to die."

One of the D and D members commented several weeks after this illness, "We knew you were fretting about not being here." She referred to a planning meeting in my home the afternoon that I was taken to the hospital. Group members were to teach the adult Sunday School classes for two weeks on *Prayer and the Spiritual Life* in celebration of Spiritual Emphasis Week. "No," I answered. "After making sure that the meeting continued without me, I never gave you another thought." So great was my trust in God and my trust in the D and Ds.

What a blessing I have been given to watch persons grow in their relationship with God. As they practice spiritual disciplines, a new trust in God develops, and a God-confidence becomes evident.

Let me explain one of the disciplines. In reading the Bible, we are using an early Christian method called *Lectio Divina*. I really believe this to be the ideal way for getting the words of Scripture from the head to the heart where lives are transformed. Basically, it follows this four-step pattern:

Lectio	which is simply reading slowly
Meditatio	meditate, think on, chew, digest
Oratio	pray the Scripture; ask the Holy Spirit what God is saying
Contemplatio	resting in the presence of God

You can see how different this is from the way we so often read, hurrying to cover a lot of pages.

Silence and solitude are two important disciplines. Solitude does not mean privacy; it means being alone with God. How we need these two disciplines, for we live in such a noisy world. The D and Ds, and now The Other Marys, meet in the Monastery of the Holy Spirit, in Conyers, Georgia, where a climate of prayer is already established. Eating in silence is perhaps the most difficult time. However, once we become adjusted to the silence, we find it restful. It is amazing how much of our energy is used for chitchat.

We need constant reminders that prayer is more than our speaking to God. The most important part of prayer is listening—allowing God to speak to us and engaging in a dialogue rather than just a monologue. When we become still and silent within, God who dwells within can be heard. Within each of us is a sanctuary of the soul. To that chapel we can return as often as we like, creating a climate of peace and stillness. To achieve the stillness of which the Psalmist speaks takes years of effort, but all of it is worthwhile—"Be still and know . . ." (Ps. 46:10a).

It is wonderful to have individual rooms to which we can retire after the times of lecture or discussion and the evening sessions. Thus, the value of what has been heard is not lost. Every discipline has a purpose of placing us before God who can then change us into the persons we are created to be.

Spiritual direction is an important part of my work with the discipleship groups. Spiritual direction is not counseling. It is more than encouragement and admonition. It is spiritual. It is concern for the whole person. Spiritual direction is needed, especially if you are directing others. How blessed I have been with a number of directors or guides along my journey. After Fr. Niel Jarreau left Atlanta for a new assignment, Fr. Augustine Moore (Fr. Gus as he is lovingly called) was willing to be my guide. He has become my friend and spiritual companion. I try to see him once a month for an hour at which time I take my journal (another discipline) and talk over questions and situations which have surfaced during the month.

It was with trepidation that I started to guide others spiritually. It comforts me to remember the words of one of my earlier mentors, Estelle Carver, who said, "If an older pilgrim on the road doesn't have something to teach young rookies, she just hasn't traveled." As to age and pilgrimage, I can qualify!

Daily, I pray for those God has sent me to lead. Perhaps the greatest lessons I have learned are the art of listening and the art of discernment. It is a wonderful thing to have the eyes of the heart opened to see what God is doing in a life and try not to interfere.

May some or all of these disciplines be helpful to you and Allen. I believe them to be essential for wholeness. To receive and give love is the greatest of all gifts. May you receive God's love and mine.

Grandmommy

Homecoming

Dear Allen And Virginia,

WHAT MAGNIFICENT BOATS ARE IN THE BAY TODAY—LARGE, elegant yachts; then, along comes a small runabout. I can't help wondering which brings the greater pleasure. For me, it is fun to pray for these strangers as they float by.

Who is God? What is God really like? Why are many children dying of starvation while others indulge in opulence? These questions plague people as they try to make sense of life. Some go merrily on their way and never take time to reflect. Others lose faith, for they can't see God's handiwork. I agree with Christopher Morley who wrote, "I had a thousand questions to ask God, but when I met him, they all fled and didn't seem to matter."

As we ponder things of the Spirit, we ask: What is God's will? If you, my dear grandchildren, have an inquisitive mind like I have, I recommend a small book entitled *The Will of God* by Leslie D. Weatherhead. It deals with what he terms:

1. The intentional will—God's ideal plan;
2. The circumstantial will—God's plan within certain circumstances; and
3. The ultimate will—God's purpose realized.

God's plan is never defeated. It may have to be delayed or altered but never defeated. God created us for intimate relationship. Disobedience causes separation. Within us is a hunger for closeness with our Creator, and we are restless until that bond is renewed.

God is a searcher, never ceasing to look for the lost ones. I love the story of the shepherd who left the ninety-nine sheep to look for the one little lost lamb. What a beautiful and accurate picture of God. Just because we disobey does not mean that God gives up on us. There is a plan for every situation. God permits us to wander far afield but trusts us to return to that intimate relationship. The whole Bible consists of episodes which demonstrate God restoring creation and bringing all people home.

What is God like? He's like the father in the story of the prodigal son. You remember the story, how the younger of the two sons wanted his inheritance before the father died. He wanted it right then. He demanded it, and the father complied. He let him have it so the boy could leave home and live it up. Then the day came when all his money was gone. The only job this young man could get was feeding swine, which, for a Jew, was beneath contempt.

Finally, his hunger and miserable condition drove him to remember home. The story says he "came to himself." He remembered who he was; he remembered his father and the loving relationship between father and son. He remembered the good things of home, the abundance of food. Even the servants had plenty to eat. Would his dad accept him? Would he let him work as a servant? With great humility, he started the homeward trek. During that long walk, he planned what he would say; he would beg for forgiveness.

How unnecessary though, for the father who had waited all those months (or was it years?) saw his son from a distance and ran with outstretched arms to welcome his son home. Quickly he directed the servants to prepare a banquet for his son who "was dead and now is alive." All the words the son had prepared were silenced. There was no tongue lashing, no reciprocity required. Instead, there was the family ring and the robe signifying family relationship. Then the neighbors were called to come and celebrate the return of the younger son.

What joy was shared by all, except for the elder brother. On hearing of this celebration, this son who had stayed home and dutifully worked for the father reacted with anger and jealousy. Enraged, he refused to attend the party. There was no celebration in his heart, only anger that the father would forget that the younger son had thrown away his inheritance, had made friends with prostitutes. When the father learned of the elder son's reaction, he hurried to speak with him. What a conversation must have taken place, what anger expressed, what jealousy revealed. Somehow, you can almost hear the pathos in the father's voice as he says, "Son, all that I have is yours."

Like the father in this story, God is unconditional love and limitless forgiveness. The joy of the Lord is restoration of relationship and of homecomings.

I was in Oroquieta City, Mindanoa, Philippines. After leading a weekend retreat alone in excessive heat, I must have looked quite weary and wistful when Perla Jalapit, my hostess, asked me if I were homesick. Recalling the distance between me and my home in Kentucky and being among people I had never met before, I considered her question and said, "Homesick?" Then words came through my lips which surprised even me, "Homesick? No, I'm home." As these words were spoken through me, an inner voice said, "When you are in me and I am in you, you are home." From that moment on, I knew that God is the homeland of my soul. Even though I have traveled many places in the world since then, when I am one with God, I am truly home. It is a wonderfully secure inner knowing.

Bless you, dear children,
Grandmother

Epilogue

IN THESE LETTERS, I HAVE ATTEMPTED TO PORTRAY THE GOD I've come to know on my long journey home. Now, I must admit: God is too deep for words.

I can write God is real, God is present, God is love. God is continuing to create; God's key word is relationship. Then I must add: *God is mystery*.

No matter how well we know God, no matter how long we've walked with Jesus, no matter how many experiences we might have had, no matter how much we've learned along the journey, we arrive at the same fact: God is beyond words; God is beyond experiences; God is inscrutable; God is mystery.

Must the fact that God is mystery cause us to throw up our hands and say, "Why seek?" Must the fact that God is inscrutable frustrate our inward journey? No, a thousand times no. It only whets our appetite. St. Paul wrote:

> So we do not lose heart. Though our outer nature is wasting away, our inner nature is being renewed every day. For this slight momentary affliction is preparing us for an eternal weight of glory beyond all comparison, because we look not to the things that are seen but to

the things that are unseen; for the things that are seen are transient, but the things that are unseen are eternal (2 Cor. 4:16–18).

In order to give human beings a tiny glimpse into mystery, God does things to and through us that are unexplainable. Let me share one of those times.

I was a speaker at a Camp Farthest Out in California. The campsite was at the foot of Mt. Lassen, and the meeting place was in an open area encircled by giant redwoods. The experience of speaking in such an inspiring setting was truly awesome. The cabins were old, rustic, and weatherbeaten. The speakers were treated to privacy, but there was no sign of beauty. The beauty was outdoors, and it was abundant. The campers were diverse and challenging.

In the breakfast line one morning, I spoke to a young woman in front of me. "I don't believe we've met. I'd like to know you," I said by way of introduction. "How I would love a conference with you," she replied. I told her that it would be fine and to set it up with Jim who was arranging my appointments.

She knocked on my cabin door that same afternoon. I discovered she was a teacher in a private high school. She was married and had one son. After these facts were recounted, she related the most horrific story I have ever heard. She informed me that she had sought psychiatric help, but it had availed nothing. She expected some answers from me.

As a spiritual guide, I never try to give advice. I only listen in love and pray. Sometimes I ask questions that might help the person find his or her own answers. This young woman's brokenness had created a wound deeper and more complex than any I had confronted. After she had poured out all the sordid details, I said, "Let us be still, then pray." I was at a total loss as to how to proceed.

In great need, I silently asked God to handle her case and the desperation she felt. Then I prayed aloud.

When I opened my eyes, I was puzzled by her weeping. She certainly did not appear to be the weeping type. When she stopped crying, she surprised me with, as best I can recall, these words: "Before I knocked on your door, I told God, if there is a God, that this woman [me] has to answer my five questions, or I will not believe a word she's said all week. You have answered all five questions."

Mystery! I neither knew the five questions nor the answers, yet her belief in God hung on those words. That God met her need in such a way remains a mystery. A year later, this same young woman drove over one hundred miles to attend a prayer workshop I was leading in Oakland, California. She told me, "I have never been the same since you answered my five questions." To this day, I have no idea what those questions were and still less, how they were answered. Mystery.

Paul said God would do more than we ask or imagine. I agree.

Love,
Grandmommy

Select Sources

MARGARET APPLEGARTH
Heirlooms

DIETRICH BONHOEFFER
Life Together

CARLO CARRETTO
Summoned by Love

RICHARD FOSTER
Celebration of Discipline

ST. IGNATIUS OF LOYOLA
The Spiritual Exercises

DAME JULIAN OF NORWICH
Revelation of Divine Love

THOMAS KELLY
Testament of Devotion

FRANK LAUBACH
Game with Minutes
Letters of a Modern Mystic

JAMES DALTON MORRISON
Masterpieces of Religious Verse

MALCOLM MUGGERIDGE
Jesus Rediscovered

EUGENE H. PETERSON
Living the Message
The Message
Where Your Treasure Is

EVELYN UNDERHILL
The Spiritual Life

LESLIE D. WEATHERHEAD
The Will of God

DALLAS WILLARD
The Spirit of the Disciplines

About the Author

MARY VIRGINIA PARRISH WAS BORN IN HOPKINSVILLE, Kentucky. She attended Bethel Women's College and Brenau University. Parrish has conducted prayer seminars and retreats in thirty-five states and numerous countries.

A frequent volunteer for church, school, and civic organizations, she served as the program director for a Hopkinsville radio station during World War II. From 1968 to 1974, she was the first executive director of the Commission on Human Relations, also in Hopkinsville.

Among the honors Parrish has received are the Woman of Achievement Award from the Business and Professional Women's Association, the Hal Thurmond Human Relations Award, and the Award of Appreciation and Honor by the North American Association of Camps Farthest Out.

The author of two previous works, *Then Comes the Joy* and *Break Out and Become*, Parrish now lives in Decatur, Georgia, where she writes and leads groups in spiritual formation.